# JOURNEY TO THE CROSS ROADS

## RANDY LEMIEUX

ISBN:  E-Book # 978-1-966556-34-3

Paperback # 978-1-966556-35-0

Printed in United States of America



Library of Congress Reg. # 2025904208

Cover Design by: Authors Hike

Publisher: Authors Hike

For permission requests, please contact: randyfitness2@gmail.com

# Table of Contents


About The Author...................................................................... i

Ode to my Mother ...................................................................... ii

Dedication .............................................................................. ii

Chapter – 1 Shadows of the Past ................................................. 1

Chapter – 2 Finding Strength in My Own Path .......................... 6

Chapter – 3 The Truths That Hurt ............................................. 10

Chapter – 4 My Multiple Pickups ............................................. 15

Chapter – 5 Turning Point – Joining the Gym........................... 22

Chapter – 6 The impact of Winston........................................... 27

Chapter – 7 Pivotal Time........................................................... 32

Chapter – 8 Taking Care of Mom.............................................. 39

Chapter – 9 Competition Days .................................................. 43

Chapter – 10 Full Circle ............................................................ 48

Chapter – 11 Passing the Torch................................................. 55

Chapter – 12 Full Circle: A Life Reclaimed.............................. 61

# About The Author

Born on August 26, 1968, Randy's life was never easy. From the moment he came into the world, he was made to feel unwanted and useless in the eyes of his father. But Randy was never one to give up. Deep inside, he carried a fire—a passion for martial arts that gave him purpose and strength.

Randy found solace in training as a teenager, dedicating himself to martial arts despite his father's disapproval. However, the constant rejection and lack of support at home led him down a dark path. Struggling with emotional pain, he fell into drug addiction, losing himself in a world that only numbed his suffering.

But fate had other plans for him. A stranger—a police officer and a few family members, including his Nana—saw potential in him when he couldn't see it in himself. Instead of treating him like a lost cause, the officer gave him a second chance, dropping him off outside Winston's gym. That moment changed everything. Under Winston's guidance, Randy found discipline, purpose, and the role model he had always longed for. Winston wasn't just a trainer; he became the father figure Randy never had, teaching him what it truly meant to be strong—not just physically, but as a man.

Randy's resilience turned his life around. The lessons from his mentor, combined with the love and wisdom of his mother, shaped him into the person he is today. Inspired by Winston, Randy always dreamed of opening his own gym—where troubled youth and passionate athletes could find guidance, just as he once did.

Through every struggle, every setback, and every triumph, Randy's journey is a testament to the power of second chances, self-belief, and the unbreakable spirit of a fighter and became a man.

# Ode to my Mother

To one who bears the sweetest name,

Adds a luster to the same,

Who shares my joys,

Who cheers me up when I'm sad,

The greatest friend I ever had,

Long life to her, for there's no other,

Can take the place of my dear mother


# Dedication

I cannot imagine my life without Winston. He has become an integral part of my life, and I cannot imagine my days without his presence, which brings joy, love, and a sense of belonging beyond description. Having such an amazing person by my side is a blessing, and I cherish our friendship beyond measure.

# Chapter – 1
# Shadows of the Past

We often consider ourselves unlucky or underprivileged when it comes to a sneak peek into our past. I am probably among them; when I look at my past, especially my childhood and teenage years, my eyes get teary.

I cherish my childhood time after that; it was hard and a lifelong lesson for me that molded me into the person I am today. We do curse our most challenging situations, but later on, we appreciate and thank them for changing us, as nothing in this world comes for free; we all have to pay the price, sometimes with money and primarily by changing ourselves or our surroundings for our betterment.

Now, people know me as a successful person, but my life was not a bed of roses; I came across a long and complicated journey in which I was shaken to my core; the only thing I did was I never ever gave up, even after many uncertain challenges.

Let churn the pages of history before my birth, when there was no planning for far to bring me into this world when my dear parents met. My parents' marriage took place in the early 1960s, and while it appeared to be a happy union to the outside world, with time, it turned out to be a conflict zone within the four boundaries.

As a man of authority and influence, my father was employed by Nortel, a firm that regularly required him to be away from family. Even though he was charismatic and adored by many people, his more sinister impulses were kept buried behind closed doors.

I came into this world in 1968, three years after my sister's birth in 1965; we were born in Montreal, Canada. Both of us were raised living under the severe control of my father. While he was home, the strain was so heavy that it was almost suffocating.

Since 1964, my mother thought my father would change after the birth of the children, but all the expectations were in vain. The anger and frustration of our father prevailed when we discovered that my elder sister was 60% deaf. According to my father, it was my mother's fault to give birth to a deaf child.

When I was a child, I had always known the guy who seemed to command both respect and dread, but it wasn't until the years began to unravel in my mind that I could truly comprehend the significance of his presence. The bond between a father and a son is strong, but in my case, it was sour.

My father was rarely home, and when he was, the tension filled the air due to his presence and negative attitude. We would see him four to six times a month, enough to mess up the peace and quiet we had treasured during his absence. His influence on our household was oppressive, and even though he was adored by many family members, it was a reality concealed from the outside world. The weight of this silence was carried by my mother, who frequently endured verbal and physical abuse that she believed she was responsible for her own actions.

In the middle of the 1970s, when I was around seven years old and my sister was 10, I had one of my earliest recollections. We went to Jamaica to be with my father, who had been working there for six months. To prevent us from falling behind in our education, my mother homeschooled us at that period as long as she received permission from the school board. The tension between my parents was always present, even though we tried to keep some semblance of normalcy in our lives. All of a sudden, that strain became apparent. A heated conversation escalated into a violent altercation, during which my father punched and choked my mother. I was only seven years old at the time, but the unexpectedness of that moment has remained with me ever since. My eyes were opened to the truth about their connection for the first time, and I felt a sense of helplessness that overwhelmed me.

I was always confused as to why my father was good to my sister but harsh with me and my mother, with time. I realized that my mother and I were the individuals who used to speak our hearts out; we used to say what we felt like without overlooking the consequences in the future; I tried to convince her that her husband and my father would make us suffer.

As time went on, I became aware of the pattern that had been established. As a result of my mother's tendency to blame herself for the assault, she would frequently assert that she had provoked him by "talking back."

At that time, I was not aware of the extent to which that belief had become ingrained in her mental disposition. Despite this, I was aware that it was a mistake. I believed that communication was the cornerstone of any relationship and that violence had no place in any relationship.

When my father was not present, our home could experience moments of peacefulness. Every time he departed for work, the house became a safe haven for my mother and me. More time was spent conversing and laughing, and for a small period, the walls of our home were no longer filled with the sound of fear.

My mother was a strong and tough woman when I was going through those difficult times. She allowed me to express my emotions, which helped me realize that talking about the suffering was acceptable rather than burying it underground. To cope with the emotional turbulence that had become a regular part of our lives, she gave me this gift to feel better.

Nevertheless, my father's shadow hovered over me even when he was not around. When my uncle was performing electrical work for my grandfather, an unforgettable event took place. My grandfather, who appreciated the assistance, presented him with a small amount of money. My father learned about it a week later and immediately became furious. It is his assertion that the family did not charge him and that he assaulted his own brother out of fury about the situation. Since they had not communicated with one another for a month, the atmosphere in the house was tense. Although my father attempted to justify his behavior, we knew it was not about money. The issue was one of control. His drive to dominate those around him, including his own family, overwhelmed his interaction with other people.

Even though the abuse became more severe as I got older, my mother never stopped forgiving him because she was convinced that it was her responsibility. Even though I will never be able to comprehend how she could rationalize his actions, I believe that some of her thought this was the inherent nature of life. On the other hand, that realization occurred to me when I was twelve years old on that particular occasion. My eyes had seen enough. I was no longer a defenseless child, and I took it upon myself to not allow him to continue to cause my mother pain without any repercussions. At some point during the night, after he had struck her once more, I confronted him. "Are you interested in engaging in combat? Fight a male opponent. I offered him a challenge by saying, "Fight me."

Everything changed as a result of that confrontation. From that moment forward, I have been his primary focus. He began to view me as a potential danger, someone who had the potential to undermine the control that he had labored so diligently to preserve. Because he considered that I posed a threat to my mother, he would reprimand me, refer to me as a disciplinary problem, and even recommend that I be sent to a military school. It was a strange situation since he, the person who caused us grief, was attempting to persuade himself that I was the danger.

Throughout our lives, my father exerted his authority over the family in every conceivable way. No one, not even our closest family, was ever informed of the abuse that we had endured. It was his method of controlling everything, ensuring that no one would ever think there was a lot of chaos in our house. From the outside, it appeared as though we were a typical family. Over many years, however, I carried the burden of those secrets with me. I did not start to make sense of everything until I found comfort in confiding in Father Victor, a family priest. Only then did I begin to understand everything. It was Father Victor who assisted me in comprehending that the abuse was not my fault; instead, it was my father's demons that had poisoned our family. Thank you for your assistance.

At approximately the same time, I began training in martial arts. I was twelve years old when I started doing it, and it quickly became my release and my method of regaining control over my life. A sense of empowerment I had never experienced before was bestowed upon me as I learned how to defend myself and became proficient in learning discipline. As a result of my instructor's willingness to acknowledge my potential, I was given the nickname "The Natural." Not only was the training physical, but it also worked on the mind. Because of it, I developed resilience, focus, and control skills, which I had long lacked in my chaotic household.

After learning that I was participating in martial arts, my father made an attempt to put me down and make me feel inferior. He glared at me and asked, "You think you're a tough guy?"

"You will never hurt me in any way. It is only the strong that survive." I chuckled, fully aware that his words could no longer influence me. My training had provided me with something significantly more valuable than the skill to fight; it had provided me with confidence.

The more I think about it, the more I realize how much that training has influenced who I am today. This experience showed me that strength is not solely about physical might; instead, it is about having control, being disciplined, and being aware of when it is appropriate to advocate for oneself and others. While it was not an easy experience for me to grow up in a household ruled by fear and control, it forced me to discover my own way. It instilled in me the wisdom to seek peace rather than confrontation and to protect rather than cause harm.

This was the path I took during my formative years, marked by forks in the road when I had to choose between fear and courage, silence and speaking up, and acquiescence and rebellion.

# Chapter – 2
# Finding Strength in My Own Path

I always found myself at odds with my father. It felt like he had some way of disapproving or belittling everything I was passionate about. The more I tried to win his approval, the more distant and harsh he seemed. My interests, particularly martial arts, were a source of contention between us. At the age of twelve, in 1980, I made a decision that would shape the course of my life—I joined martial arts. It was the first time I chose something for myself, despite knowing it would go against my father's wishes.

Growing up, I was captivated by Bruce Lee. His style was effortless, flawless, and powerful, and I wanted to be like him. But it wasn't just admiration; there was a deeper reason. I wanted to protect my mother. My father's dominance over our family was stifling, especially for her. He not only physically hurt her, but his words and attitude were oppressive, too. He was loud, controlling, and never open to suggestions, particularly from me or my mother. He liked to have the final say in everything, and that left my mom with little choice but to endure.

Martial arts gave me something to focus on, something that was mine. My father, however, wasn't impressed. In fact, he was angry. He wanted me to follow in the footsteps of my cousins, who were all hockey players. Hockey was his sport, even though he'd never played it himself. It seemed like my father's greatest joy was undermining anything I liked, and hockey was no different. I tried to play for his sake, but I wasn't any good. It wasn't that I didn't like hockey—it just wasn't for me. My lack of interest showed in every game, and it only gave my father more bombs.

"You're not meeting my expectations," he would say over and over again, comparing me to my cousins as though they were the zenith of success.

When he came to one of my hockey practices, my coach, trying to offer encouragement, said, "Your boy has great strength." Instead of feeling proud, my father seemed to take it as an insult. In his mind, there was no room for compliments unless they were about how well I could handle a puck. He hit the coach. Right there, in front of everyone. I stood frozen, embarrassed, and angry but not surprised. My father couldn't tolerate anyone giving me praise, especially for something he disapproved of.

Martial arts, on the other hand, brought me peace. Every time I learned a new move or mastered a technique, I felt stronger—not just physically, but emotionally. I would come home and show my family what I had learned. My mother was always supportive. She would smile and tell me how proud she was. My sister, though she watched with curiosity, kept her distance. She was much closer to my father, and in her eyes, he could do no wrong. It wasn't her fault. My father treated her like she was his little princess, giving her special attention while pushing me aside.

Whenever I demonstrated my martial arts moves, my father's usual response was, "You can't beat me up." He would laugh as if to challenge me, but his words stung. Every time, I would reply, "Self-defense," and move on. Deep down, I knew those words gave my mother strength. She felt safer knowing I was learning how to protect myself and possibly her. But I could also see the sadness in my sister's eyes. To her, I was defying the man she saw as a hero.

Our family dynamic was always strained. My father was away during the week, busy with work, but his presence hung over us even when he wasn't home. When the weekends rolled around, we would all brace ourselves for his outbursts. His controlling nature made it impossible for anyone to voice their opinions. He shut down any suggestion from me or my mom simply to assert his dominance.

When the extended family came over for gatherings, I always hoped for the moment that martial arts would come up. My uncles would show interest, asking me about what I was learning and even praising me. I could see their genuine curiosity and pride. But without fail, my father would steer the conversation elsewhere. He would go out of his way to make me feel guilty as if my passion for martial arts was some kind of betrayal. "He should be playing hockey," he'd say. It was like he wanted to erase the things that made me unique.

I found solace in my friendships. We had a close-knit group of about twenty friends, all from school and the neighborhood. With them, I could escape from the tension at home. We spent our time hanging out at the mall, going to movies, or just driving around, enjoying each other's company. I practically lived at their houses sometimes, just to get away from my father's relentless criticism. But no matter how much fun I had with them, the worry for my mother was always in the back of my mind.

On the other hand, I frequently took my younger cousins to martial arts classes with me to show them who I was. They were impressed with my abilities and how I was doing dojo.

I never told my friends about what was going on at home. To them, I was just Randy, the guy who loved martial arts and was always up for a laugh. I wanted to keep it that way. Sharing my family issues felt too personal, and besides, I didn't want to seem weak.

Martial arts had taught me strength, but it also taught me discipline. I learned how to control my emotions, how to focus, and most importantly, how to stand up for myself in ways that didn't involve fighting.

My mother was my anchor. She had a quiet wisdom about her, always offering me advice that I knew came from a place of love and experience. "Don't judge people," she would say. "Only God can judge people." Her words resonated with me, especially as I grew older and saw how differently my parents viewed the world. My mother believed that everyone had good and bad in them, but it was a person's heart that mattered most. She would often remind me, "If you have a good heart, you're a good person."

My father, on the other hand, had a more rigid and, frankly, prejudiced outlook. He judged people by their skin color, something I couldn't understand or agree with. His narrow-mindedness was one of the many things that drove a wedge between us. While my mother taught me to listen to my heart and see the humanity in everyone, my father seemed consumed by his need to control and judge.

As the years went on, I held on to my mother's teachings. They became the guiding principles in my life, shaping how I viewed the world and interacted with others. I refused to let my father's harsh judgments define me or how I treated people. The lessons I learned in martial arts helped me stay grounded. It was about more than just fighting or defending myself—it was about building inner strength, something my father could never take away from me.

Despite the constant tension at home, I never stopped practicing martial arts. It was my escape, my passion, and ultimately, my way of standing up to my father. While he continued to push hockey on me, I found peace in following my own path. I knew deep down that I didn't need his approval to be happy. What mattered was that I was becoming the person I wanted to be—a person who could protect the ones he loved, who believed in kindness and fairness, and who, thanks to his mother's wisdom, saw the good in people, no matter their background.

In the end, my journey wasn't about winning my father's acceptance. It was about learning to accept myself and to find strength in the things I loved, regardless of anyone else's expectations.

# Chapter – 3
# The Truths That Hurt

At the age of fourteen, after years of devoting myself to martial arts and putting in a lot of effort, I was finally on the verge of accomplishing something that I had dreamed of for years: earning my black belt.

It is possible that for someone else, this might have been a stepping stone; rather, for me, it was a symbol of strength, endurance, and a quiet victory over the constant critiques that my father has directed on me.

Discipline, focus, and a sense of purpose were all things that I sorely needed in a family where I frequently felt like I was not seen or heard. My training had provided me with all of these things.

The black belt ceremony was a very important event. It was going to be a major ceremony where I would receive my black belt from Hanshi: master of masters, and I would be surrounded by my classmates and teachers who had seen my development throughout my physical education.

Despite the fact that I was ecstatic, a cloud of uncertainty lingered over my head. The members of my family were not going to be around to see me reaching this significant milestone. During the entire ceremony, my father was not present. Because he was preoccupied with attending a hockey tournament for my cousin, he was totally oblivious to the fact that this day was really important to me. At that point, I had become accustomed to his carelessness, but it still stung. Despite the fact that my mother was aware of the event, she was preoccupied with household tasks. How about my sister? Instead of showing her support for me, she rather went to a hockey game with her buddies and hung out with them.

The fact that my family was not present on such a significant day caused me to feel a profound and distressing sense of loss. As I stood there in my martial arts costume, collecting my black belt award, surrounded by praise and cheers from people I did not know, the only thing that I could think about was how isolated I felt. They regarded it as nothing more than another ritual. Personally, it was the result of years of labor that I had put in. I had pictured my family waiting there, beaming with pride to see me, but unfortunately, I was standing there by myself.

I couldn't wait to present my father with my black belt when he came back to the house two weeks later. I had the hope that he would observe how far I had progressed and, for once, be proud of me. I believe that this is possible.

On the other hand, his expression remained ice-cold even after I handed him the black belt. Nothing, not even a reaction, was noticed. It felt as if my accomplishment was devoid of any significance at all. In point of fact, rather than applauding me, he asked me in his typical condescending manner, "From which store did you got it?"

"From China," I responded, attempting to conceal the growing rage that was building up within me.

His comments struck a chord deep within. My black belt was nothing more than a waste of time in his eyes; it was nothing more than a collection of battles wrapped up in a piece of paper. Neither did he care about what it meant to me, nor did he try to comprehend it. My lack of appreciation from him made me feel as though all of my hard work and achievements were for nothing, and it made me feel worthless. The nonstop demeaning, the never-ending comparisons to my relatives, and the idea that I could never be good enough in his eyes were all factors that contributed to this sentiment. However, this particular moment was not the only problem.

I was unable to continue to handle the emotional burden that I was carrying. It had always been the case that my father's control threw a shadow over our home, but now I felt as though I was being suffocated by it. When I was in search of an escape, a means to dull the ache of never being accepted, my friends introduced me to marijuana. I found that it was just what I needed. To begin, it was nothing more than a simple plan to spend some time with the boys and temporarily forget about the issues that I was concerned about. Our location was at a sports complex in the neighborhood, where they were practicing football. At the age of fourteen, I was oblivious to the danger. As a young person, I was bewildered and in urgent need of something to alleviate the pain that was in my heart.

But marijuana quickly evolved into something more than just a method to relax. It became my means of evading the realities of life. When my father insulted me or neglected me, I would go away into the blur of drugs, where I would forget about it all and pretend that it didn't matter anymore. This group of pals did not pass judgment on me. The fact that they were in the same situation as us, attempting to find solutions to their problems, gave the impression that we were all in this together for a time. However, as time went on, I began to spiral out of control.

On a particular day, my father extended an invitation to a few of his close friends to attend a private celebration that would take place at our residence. As is his custom, he was drinking extensively and was trapped in a state that was somewhere between consciousness and hypnosis. When we were in the middle of our chat, he turned to me, laughed cruelly, and said, "You were the biggest mistake of my life."

Like a sledgehammer, his remarks struck the target. Unable to contain their horror at what they had just heard, everyone fell silent. At that moment, my father suddenly burst out laughing as if he were attempting to downplay the gravity of what he had just spoken. However, the harm had already been done. Even though he laughed, what he had said was not forgotten. The flame that he had stoked in my heart was not extinguished, no matter what.

In utter devastation, I stood there. After the event, my mother, who was constantly trying to make things more cordial, took me aside and said, "Your father didn't mean it." Just to grab people's attention, he was kidding around. But I was aware that it wasn't a joke at all. The truth was revealed. He considered me to be an error. Despite the fact that my mother made numerous attempts to console me, the words continued to play over and over in my thoughts.

My sense of self-awareness began to fade just at that instant. The use of marijuana could no longer alleviate the discomfort. At the same time that I began experimenting with stronger drugs, I began to lose track of who I was and what I desired. I had been in a downward spiral for two and a half years. As a result of my absence from school, I got into fights and got into trouble. Eventually, I was kicked out of one school for fighting, and I had to enroll in another school in order to complete my education. I was a disaster by the time I graduated from high school at the age of eighteen; I was a shadow of the boy I used to be.

I was able to feel wonderful after using drugs, or at the very least, they prevented me from feeling anything at all. It was no longer important to consider the world beyond. Even the insults from my father and the absence of my family vanished while I was under the influence of drugs. As a result of my bullying behavior toward other students at school, I became someone I could not even recognize. My friends began to refer to me as "Crazy Randy" due to the fact that I became extremely irresponsible while I was under the influence of drugs. Everyone, including those who attempted to assist me, was pushed away by me.

Attempts were made to stop me from following this course of action by one of my closest friends, who had been there for me throughout my whole life. He observed the effects that the medications were having on me and made an effort to intervene. When I was in a high and warped condition, however, I regarded him as my enemy.

In the end, I broke up with him, severing all ties with the one person who had genuine concern for me. When I finally came to terms with what I had done, it was a very long time later. He was merely attempting to be of assistance.

I dove deeper into the world of drugs, selling them to other people in order to make some additional money. I didn't think twice about accepting the narcotics that the leader of the gang handed me to sell at the collegiate level. I resided in my own world, governed by my own set of laws. The consequences were irrelevant to me at the time. Finding a method to get away from the agony that I was experiencing on the inside was the only thing that mattered to me. I turned to drugs as a form of therapy and a means of coping with the emotional upheaval that I was experiencing at the time. My name was no longer Randy; I was nothing more than a shell that was concealed by the cloud of narcotics.

My mother has observed this in me. She witnessed me escaping home, skipping school, and getting into trouble despite my best efforts. There was not much that she could do to assist despite her best efforts. My father had given up on me and was always referring to me as a failure. His comments continued to reverberate in my thoughts, which fueled my desire to flee even further.

My buddies, or more precisely, the dads of my friends, were among the police officers who attempted to interfere in the situation. In an effort to deter me from engaging in drug use, they would go and pick me up in their vehicles. He informed me of the risks, the adverse consequences, and the damage that would occur over the long run. But I choose not to pay attention. My concern for the future was nonexistent. In the here and now, the only thing that mattered to me was numbing the pain.

Reflecting on the past, I am able to see how far I have fallen. When I was looking for acceptance, I was hunting in all the wrong places, and I was furious, sad, and lost. Drugs did not fill the hole that I felt inside; rather, they just made it larger. As a result of my actions, I became estranged from the individuals who cared about me and turned against those who attempted to assist me.

However, despite the fact that I was under the influence of drugs and fury, there was still a small part of me that desired to improve and that desired to discover a way out. It would take me a number of years to come to the realization that the approval I had been looking for all along was not something I required from my father or anybody else. It was something that existed within me that I needed to discover.

# Chapter – 4
# My Multiple Pickups

Individuals who are in their late teenage years typically experience a period of self-discovery, aspirations, and excitement for the future. Those years, on the other hand, were a haze of confusion for me, fueled by drugs and fights that I couldn't seem to help but get involved in. I was drifting between moments of wild enjoyment and brutal reality, and despite the fact that my life was strengthening out of control, I was somehow invulnerable to the aftermaths.

At this point, the local cops had a very good understanding of who I was. In their lives, I had developed into something of a constant presence. Despite the fact that they would pick me up again and over again, I was never arrested or taken to jail. I never got the chance to see the face of jail. I am not sure if it is good or bad. It wasn't clear to me whether that was a positive or negative thing to happen.

Possibly, they recognized something in me that I was unable to recognize in myself. They probably thought I wasn't hopeless and that, hidden beneath the drugs and fights, there was the "well-mannered" youngster they all knew before I started down this tarnished path.

The majority of my interactions with law enforcement officers followed the same pattern. The majority of the time, I would get into fights with other males who were just as high as I was. Drugs were the most common cause of the fights, which were not random in nature.

A few of these guys were under the impression that they could get marijuana or other substances from me at no cost. On the other hand, I was not managing a charitable organization. As a result of the fact that drugs had become my source of additional income, I was not going to give them away to anyone who refused to pay on time. Consequently, when they were unable to pay for the item, the situation became heated, and it invariably resulted in blows being thrown.

Especially when I was high, there was something about the surge of adrenaline that came with fighting that I found particularly enjoyable.

I did not just engage in combat; rather, I utilized my skills in martial arts to gain the upper hand. Despite the fact that they were not always under control, every punch and kick was calculated. My perceptions were numbed by the medicines, but muscle memory began to take effect. This was a harsh irony if you will remember it. At this precise moment, I was exploiting the very thing that had once provided me with a sense of purpose and calm.

As the confrontations continued to develop, the police eventually arrived to put an end to them. That is how my life was. In the beginning, the other males would disperse among themselves like terrified animals, scurrying in every direction in an attempt to avoid being captured. Not so with me. During the time that they were running towards the shadows, I started walking. Slowly, in fact. Relaxedly. As if I didn't give a damn about it. It could have been my self-assurance, it could have been my foolishness, or it could have been the medicines I was under that were clouding my judgment. In any case, I was aware that the authorities would eventually find me and arrest me. It was always the case.

I found it amusing that they did not have to go out of their way to find me. When they arrived, they would simply pull up next to me, roll down the window, and inquire, "Hey Randy, what are you doing?" We were so familiar with each other that it was almost as if we knew one other by our first names. Moreover, rather than reacting in a manner that is typical of a human, I would begin to utter vulgar language and curses in their direction. They were aware that I was not in my right mind at the time. My statements were not taken by them as a personal attack. They would approach me, grab me, and force me into the back of their police cruiser, where they would then attempt to talk some sense into me.

In particular, I can recall one police officer, the father of my student, whom I used to teach martial arts. Prior to my descent into drug addiction, I had instructed his son in some fundamental martial arts techniques. When I was younger, he was aware of the fact that I had changed, and he was able to see through the mess that I had become. That one day, after picking me up for what seemed like the hundredth time, he said something that struck me with a great deal of force.

It was when we were driving through the peaceful neighborhoods that he made the statement, "Randy, you are two different people." I was confused about what he wanted to say.

He judged that I was confused with my statement, "My child learns how to defend himself from you when you are not under the influence of drugs because you are a calm and disciplined young man. You are a complete and utter mess when you are high. Like you don't care about anything or anyone, that's what it seems like."

I have not forgotten what he said. It had been a very long time since I had actually started to think about the person I used to be, the young boy who was passionate about martial arts and who found meaning in every kick and punch, not with the intention of inflicting harm on others but rather to achieve equilibrium inside himself.

During my training, I used to experience a sense of pride. More than just a skill; it was a means by which I could regain my composure and go away from the chaos that was occurring at home with my father. But I was no longer that guy at that point in time. In the midst of a sea of drugs and violence, I found myself lost, and I had no idea how to return back to the person I had been before.

Simultaneously, there was one particular occurrence that struck me, and I will never forget it. I was involved in yet another altercation with a group of individuals who refused to compensate me for the drugs that I had brought to them. As the cops arrived, I was tossed into the back of a squad car and taken into custody. This time, it was the same police officer, who was also the father of the young man that I had previously instructed. He did not reprimand me or attempt to give me a lecture while we were driving in quiet. Rather than that, he turned his attention to me and stated, "I am aware that this is not who you are, Randy."

I was taken aback by that straightforward comment, which struck me like a blow to the stomach. Deep down, I was aware that he was correct. The issue was that I had lost myself and had no idea who I was anymore. Because I had allowed myself to become so engrossed in my own suffering and anguish, I had lost track of the person I had been in the past.

The drugs were not the only thing at issue. It was everything: the continual battles, the upheaval at home with my father, and the way my mother fought to keep things together as I watched her suffer in silence. It was everything. It was an excessive amount. It was only the medicines that were able to prevent me from remembering. Nevertheless, at the same time, they were completely tearing me apart from the inside out.

My passion for martial arts began to wane, and I began to become aware of this fact. It used to be the thing that made me happy and gave me the impression that I had some degree of control over my life until recently. Now, it seemed like a recollection from a long time ago. I was not training as frequently as I had been. I continued to teach a few students here and there, but I no longer felt the same level of enthusiasm. My heart felt hollow as if a piece of me had been taken away, and I was at a loss for how to fill the emptiness that it left behind.

In point of fact, martial arts had offered me a sense of fulfillment in the past, but the drugs had deprived me of that. Instead of confronting my issues head-on, I turned to psychoactive substances as a means of evading them. The incessant ridiculing that I received from my father, the apathy that I received from my sister, and the pressure that I felt to live up to the expectations of another person all weighed on me. And I used the pills as a means of avoiding experiencing any of it anymore.

Martial arts used to satisfy my soul, but the intake of drugs used to get rid of all the tensions that were coming over me due to my family situation.

On the other hand, the cops kept following me around, and each time they did so, they made an effort to warn me. I was not being threatened with incarceration in an attempt to frighten me; rather, they were attempting to communicate with me in order to make me realize that I was heading down a path that would only result in my own demise. They explained to me how narcotics were progressively destroying me from the inside out and how they were eating away at me. I listened to what they had to say, but I felt as though I was unable to make myself care.

After one of these run-ins, a law enforcement officer who was familiar with me and had had the opportunity to pick me up on multiple occasions approached me and stated, "You know, Randy, we're not trying to ruin your fun right now." We are making an effort to conserve your life.

At that moment, I was able to laugh it off. My desire was to avoid hearing it. I didn't want to give any thought to the repercussions that would result from what I was doing. However, the reality is that I was already experiencing its effects. My body and my mind were beginning to feel the effects of the medications that I was taking. My skills in martial arts were starting to deteriorate. I'm not as quick or as concentrated as I used to be. I'm much slower. Despite the fact that I was not high, I was able to sense that something was incorrect.

I had a sense that I was losing control of my own life, and I had an empty feeling inside of me. During my fights, I came to the realization that I was not fighting other people, but rather I was fighting myself. I was irritated, emotional, and perplexed. On top of that, rather than confronting those feelings, I buried them further deeper with each hit, each pill, and each line.

The people who were around me, particularly the law enforcement officers who knew me, did not give up. I was constantly being picked up and talked to by them, and they were attempting to convince me that I was more capable than this. Although they could put me in jail, they chose not to do so. It's possible that they recognized the potential in me, or it's also likely that they simply believed that I wasn't that hopeless. No matter what the rationale was, they continued to show up.

With the benefit of hindsight, I am able to see that those interactions with law enforcement were more than mere warnings. The events in question served as wake-up calls, occasions that compelled me to face the truth about my state of life. I did not have any appreciation for it at the time. Not only was I too preoccupied with my personal sorrow, but I was also too preoccupied with the drugs and the conflicts that I was unable to recognize what was happening to me. However, I have come to the realization that they were attempting to assist me in seeing something that I was unable to see for myself, which was that I was gradually losing everything that made me who I was.

And even though I didn't completely get it at the time, those multiple pickups were the beginning of something. Those were the experiences that caused the wall that I had constructed around myself to begin to break. It was all driving me to a breaking point, a moment when I would finally have to face the person I had become and decide whether I wanted to continue down this path or find a way to turn my life around. The cops, the fights, and the drugs were all contributing factors.

At 16, one late Saturday night, I was abruptly awakened by a sound that shook me to my core—my mother screaming for help. I rushed to their bedroom, my heart racing, and as I kicked the door open, I saw my father pinning her down, his hands wrapped around her neck, choking her. My mother's desperate eyes met mine, pleading for me to save her. Without thinking, I grabbed a baseball bat and charged in.

Adrenaline took over as I swung the bat, forcing my father off of her. We fought—hard. I had never been that furious before, and I could feel the intensity of the moment taking over my actions. In the chaos, I threw my father through my sister's bedroom door. The noise woke her up, and before she even understood what was happening, she jumped onto my back, thinking I was attacking him. She didn't realize I was trying to protect our mother.

That night felt like a nightmare, but it was all too real. I couldn't stay there after that. Early the next morning, I packed a bag and left to stay with friends, unsure if I'd ever return. I couldn't face what had happened, and I definitely didn't want to be around my father.

By Monday, my mother called me at my friend's house. She begged me to come home, saying that my father had apologized and promised he would change. He was leaving for a job that would keep him away for a week or two, so I agreed to return. Part of me hoped that maybe this time, things would be different. But deep down, I knew better.

When I got back, the dynamic in the house had shifted. I begged my mother to leave him. I told her she deserved better, that this wasn't a life anyone should have to live. But she repeated the same things she always said—that he was sweet deep down, that he was truly sorry this time, and that he promised things would be different. I wanted to believe her, but I knew I couldn't.

When my father returned from his job, he was surprised to see me back home. There was an unspoken tension between us. I didn't hide my feelings—I told him, "Somebody has to protect Mom." That was the only thing I said to him, and nothing more was mentioned about what had happened that night.

The incident left a mark on me. It was a moment that showed me the horror of the situation we were living in, and it solidified the fact that I couldn't trust my father's apologies or my mother's hope that he would change. It was a harsh reality to face, but it was one I had to live with. The fear, the anger, and the helplessness of that night stayed with me, shaping the way I saw the world and my place in it.

# Chapter – 5
# Turning Point – Joining the Gym

After what felt like my millionth arrest, I was sick of it all. I was bored of the same routine—getting caught, being lectured, and then released.

Each time, I went back to the same bad habits, and each time, the cops would tell me the same things: "You're wasting your life," and "You need to turn things around." Their words went in one ear and out the other. But one day, something different happened.

This particular police officer, who had picked me up again after a fight while I was high, asked me what I actually wanted to do with my life. It was a strange question, one I hadn't been asked before, and for a moment, I didn't know what to say.

Then, almost instinctively, I told him, "I want to do weightlifting and martial arts."

The officer smiled at me in a way I hadn't seen before. It wasn't the usual look of disappointment or frustration I was used to. It was like he saw something in me that I couldn't see myself. After a pause, he dropped me off in front of a tall office building and said, "Go up to the second floor. There's a gym there. Join it. Change your life."

As I got out of the car, he gave me one last piece of advice. "Either you turn your life around, or two things will happen: you'll end up in jail, or worse, dead." His words hit me like a punch. He wasn't just saying it for effect—he meant it.

I climbed the stairs to the second floor, unsure of what to expect. I had on a t-shirt and some raggedy pants, ready to fight anyone who came my way. I was angry, defensive, and full of unresolved tension. But when I reached the gym's door, all of that shifted.

Standing in the doorway was a massive figure. A black man, at least 6'2", and 275 pounds of solid muscle. His presence was commanding, but instead of looking intimidating, he smiled and greeted me warmly. "Welcome, son!" he said.

I was taken aback. No one had ever called me "son" before. The word felt foreign but comforting. It made me defensive at first. Was this guy mocking me? But something about his tone made it clear that he wasn't. His name was Winston, and he had this natural charisma that made people listen to him.

I told him I was just visiting the gym, not intending to join right away. It's Winston's energy, his confidence, and his genuine interest in me made me rethink that. He walked me around the gym, showing me the equipment and introducing me to some of the regulars.

Everyone seemed to know him, and as we walked, people were giving me curious looks. Maybe they sensed I didn't belong there yet, but Winston didn't care. He treated me like I did.

There was something about this place that felt right. The air smelled of sweat and determination. The sound of weights clanging, people grunting through reps, and trainers shouting encouragement—it was a symphony of effort, and I found myself wanting to be a part of it.

We passed by a studio, and inside was a sleek, heavy bag. I made a joke about it, and Winston's booming laugh filled the space. I didn't know it then, but that moment was the start of something big for me. Winston asked, "Do you box?"

"No, I do martial arts."

He smiled even bigger. "Good," he said. "You'll fit right in."

I joined the gym that day without hesitating. The membership was $200 a year, a price I would have hesitated at in the past, but now, it felt like the best investment I could make.

I went home that night and told my mom all about it. I told her how Winston's energy pulled me in, how, for the first time in a long while, I felt like I had a place I wanted to be.

The first thing I did after joining the gym was quit drugs. Cold turkey. I told myself if I was going to do this, if I was going to turn my life around, I had to stop poisoning my body. For once, I actually followed through on a promise I made to myself. The gym became my new addiction.

Within the first week, I was already talking to new people. These weren't the usual crowd I hung out with, the guys always looking for their next fix or trying to score some quick cash. These were people who were driven and who had goals. Winston was at the center of it all. He wasn't just a trainer; he was a leader, a mentor.

One day, he told me something that stuck with me: "Forget the bad in people. Focus on the good." At first, it was hard for me to grasp. My life had been filled with so much negativity—fights, drugs, my father's endless criticism—that it felt impossible to let it go. But with Winston's guidance, I slowly started to shift my perspective.

Despite the changes I was making, my father remained a constant source of bitterness. He hated the idea of me associating with people like Winston, making racist remarks and trying to convince me that I'd never belong. But I knew better. Winston wasn't just some gym owner. He was a good man, and I was learning more from him than I ever had from my father.

With time, the gym became my sanctuary. I had a routine—martial arts training, lifting weights, going to work as a dishwasher, and studying. It was far from glamorous, but it gave my life structure. For the first time in years, I felt like I was in control of something.

Physically, I transformed. I went from being a lean, scrappy kid to someone with real muscle mass. People at the gym started noticing, and soon, I wasn't just the new guy anymore. I was one of them. Winston took me under his wing, teaching me techniques and encouraging me to keep pushing myself. He never doubted me, and that belief made me strive to be better.

One afternoon, as I was finishing up a session, I saw a 6.4' in height, weight around 300 pounds man enter the gym. He looked rough—shattered in a way I hadn't seen someone; I was just a boy then, still, I was able to figure out he was determined yet confused with his situation. His face was saying everything. His eyes were hollow, he spoke softly. He approached me, and before I could ask what was wrong, he muttered, "You are Randy? You're the new kid in the gym."

"Yes, I am Randy," I said in a confused voice; I was not sure how he knew my name and why he was asking me.

"My name is Mike, and I heard from Winston that you can teach me some techniques in martial arts that could be beneficial to me as a doorman."

I frowned at him. Confused, I asked him, "How can martial arts techniques benefit him as a doorman?"

I didn't want to break his heart, so I casually replied, "That's great, but first grab me as if you are going to escort me out of the club, as I put my hands behind my back."

As I told him, he stepped forward, and with both hands, he proceeded to grab me at the opening of my collar.

I sidestepped him just by taking a step with my right foot backward, which put him off balance. I rolled my shoulder into his extended arms, breaking the hold. He was taller than me, and he was confused by this step I had taken, but at the same time, he was happy, too.

I told him, "Never underestimate your opponent."

Actually, it was a forceful grab by him, yet not painful for me. What I saw in his eyes was passion and determination. Mike and I exchanged a few words, and he went away. Later, I realized I had seen him a few times as a security guard—actually, a doorman at Winston Churchill Night Club. I had passed by him casually, and he was always a quiet person.

As time went on, I realized that joining the gym had been the turning point I needed. It wasn't just about lifting weights or practicing martial arts. It was about finding purpose, finding discipline, and finding a community that cared about me in a way I hadn't experienced before.

On the other hand, Winston became more than just a mentor—he filled the void left by my father's absence. Where my father belittled me, Winston lifted me up. Where my father saw my efforts as a waste of time, Winston saw potential. And that made all the difference.

Coming back to Mike, when he went with a great smile, I met Winston around an hour later; we both were talking casually while walking, and I was unable to resist; I asked Winston, "Why did Mike approach me about learning the techniques?"

"I told him to approach you."

"Why me? I am just a beginner."

Winston stopped, took a deep breath, and said, "I know you can only do this."

This statement of his made me confused; why me? There are many other well-trained people around; why he suggested my name? I was confused about what I should say or ask from Winston.

Winston was a man of wisdom; he used to understand things without words, as he was unable to ask what he wanted to say, so he analyzed it on his own; he held my hand and said, "In my hand is a lump of coal and It is my job to chip away at the piece of coal and draw out the most brilliant diamond for the world to see and that diamond is YOU!"

He stopped for a few seconds; I was blank, don't know how to react or what to say; he continued, "I see potential in you, and you can achieve anything you put your mind to."

There was a spark in his eyes and a hope from me, which was evident; he touched me emotionally. I always wanted this type of support from my parents, to hear praise and appreciation from them, but unfortunately, I was deprived of but Winston filled the gap by trusting and motivating me; he was just a stranger sent by God in my life.

# Chapter – 6
# The impact of Winston

Whenever I walked into Winston's gym, it was like stepping into a completely different world. It developed into a community and a family, in addition to being a location where people could go to lift weights or practice martial arts. At the core of it all was Winston, who served not only as a guide but also as a representation of a father figure that I had never had.

Over time, I ended up developing a strong relationship with Mike, too, who was seven years older than me. I was just 16 years old, and Mike was 23 years old when we first met; he treated me as if I were on the same footing as him. The first five years of our relationship were spent as a teacher and student, with me assisting him in refining his skills. However, as time went on, he became more like a big brother to me, and we spent the entire time pushing one another to our limits.

When Mike initially started the gym, he was somewhat reserved and isolated. On the other hand, after a year of working together, he began to become more open. Because of our connection, he was able to come out of his bubble and start sharing things with me, particularly during our coffee, which we used to have often after our workout.

One afternoon, he revealed something to me that took me by surprise: Mike was completely obsessed with cooking. His job as a security guard did not provide him with any genuine happiness; what he truly desired was to work in the culinary industry.

I cheered him on with all my heart and assured him that I would be there for him at every single stage of the process. Our friendship was sincere, and we both wished for the best for one another. We had each other's backs, and our faith in one another was unbreakable.

Mike revealed yet another shocking revelation while he was enjoying a cup of coffee close to the workplace. Winston was not only the proprietor of the club, but he was also a former head judge for the International Federation of Bodybuilding and Fitness (IFBB) and a close friend of the famed Joe and Ben Weider. Bodybuilding legends such as Arnold Schwarzenegger, Frank Zane, and Franco Columbu were among the individuals that Winston had evaluated. Hearing these names was a strange experience. I had seen these guys in publications and admired their physiques, and here was Winston, connected to them in ways that I could not have imagined.

While I was attempting to take everything in, I stared at Mike. Throughout his whole life, Winston had never once boasted about his connections or revealed his history. To me, he was just Winston; he was the person who greeted me with open arms and believed in me when they did not believe in anybody else.

Once, in response to my questioning him about it, he merely shrugged his shoulders and remarked, "Yes, it is true. However, my name is Winston. I've been fortunate enough to have some opportunities, and I've had the pleasure of meeting wonderful individuals, but it doesn't alter who I am."

As time went on, I realized that Winston was the kind of person who treated everyone with respect, regardless of who they were or where they came from. He was a remarkable individual. It was the type of kindness and acceptance that I had never experienced before that he showed me when he let me into his life and into his gym. His words of encouragement and the fact that he referred to me as "a gift" left an impression on me. Even before I had finished speaking, he was already aware of what I was going to say; it was almost as if he could read my mind. For some reason, he was able to recognize something in me that no one else could.

When I first started going to the gym, there were a few individuals who were doubtful about my relationship with Winston and Mike. The fact that they saw me as a small child receiving special treatment from the proprietor of the gym appeared to irritate a considerable number of individuals. They did not understand the link that I enjoyed with these two men, and I frequently felt the judgmental gazes that they directed upon me. However, I did not care. I couldn't have any doubts about Winston and Mike because they were both extremely important in my life.

On a certain Saturday, Pat and Bernie, two of my cousins, traveled all the way from Toronto to come and visit me. I saw this as the ideal occasion to show them Winston's gym and provide them with some advice because both of them were hockey players. My goal was to provide them with genuine training that would be beneficial to them not just in their sport but also in their everyday lives. People were greeting me as we entered the gym, and my cousins were clearly astonished by what they saw.

We immediately began a leg workout, and Winston came by in the middle of the exercise. When I introduced him to Pat and Bernie, he greeted them with the same warmheartedness that he always does. He congratulated me by tapping me on the back and saying, "You are being trained by the best." "You're doing great, Champ?" Although they didn't say much, I could see that my cousins were having a good time during the session.

However, by the following day, both of them were incomprehensibly uncomfortable. They were jokingly criticizing me for putting them through that workout since they were so weak that they could not move. My heart jumped with joy as I welcomed them into my life.

However, my father reacted in a manner that was quite different from what I expected. As soon as he became aware of their discomfort, he accused me of being an ineffective trainer, implying that I may have put their hockey careers in danger by overworking them.

As usual, he found a way to confuse the situation by presuming the worst possible thing about me. The hard reality that he would never see me in a different light, regardless of how much I improved, was brought home to me by this one.

Something very remarkable took place in the year 1985. Hulk Hogan arrived in town, and the World Wrestling Federation gave Winston the responsibility of driving him. Winston was trusted to take care of Hulk by the World Wrestling Federation (now known as WWE), which had strict security protocols. For the purpose of providing Hulk with a peaceful environment in which to exercise, Winston decided to close the gym for the day. He then hired Mike and me to watch the door, ensuring that Hulk's workout was uninterrupted by anyone. It felt like a dream to be able to watch Hulk Hogan work out in person. He demonstrated the kind of dedication that only a select few people have by training for a continuous period of three hours.

However, that was not the end of it. I was summoned into Winston's office a few days later, and there I found none other than Joe Weider, the president of the International Federation of Bodybuilding and Fitness (IFBB). They were talking about an upcoming seminar that will be held with Lee Haney, who is now the reigning Mr. Olympia and a legend in the world of bodybuilding. Simply hearing those names—Hulk Hogan, Joe Weider, and Lee Haney—made me feel as though I was living in a make-believe world.

1986 was the year that the seminar took place, and it was much more overwhelming than I could have possibly thought it would be. There were a lot of individuals in the gym who were enthusiastic about meeting Lee Haney in person, and the atmosphere in the room was very exciting. The presentation that Haney gave was quite educational. He discussed the virtues of self-control, diet, and training, as well as the commitment that was required to achieve success. After that, there was a private refreshment session for the essential guests, and as Lee left, he gave Winston a huge hug as a sign of respect for the one who had been a part of his journey till that point.

When I saw a man I had only seen on television and in publications standing there in person, I was filled with respect and admiration. Lee Haney was a great champion, even though he was a humble and powerful individual. The extent to which these champions admired Winston, not only for his competence but also for his character, impacted me.

Throughout everything that happened, Winston continued to serve as a guide for me, not only in the gym but also in life. He inspired me to search for the positive qualities in other people and to look past their shortcomings. "Forget the bad, Randy," he would tell them, "and concentrate on the good."

It was not easy, especially considering that my father appeared to be unrelenting in his efforts to bring me down. On the other hand, under Winston's direction, I started to see things in a different light.

When I was out and about, people would stop me to inquire about Winston, and even the most accomplished businesspeople would tell me, "Tell Winston that I treated you right." The influence of his reputation was so great that people from all walks of life looked up to him and revered him.

In addition to being a location where I could grow muscle, the gym became a place where I learned resiliency, loyalty, and respect for another person. My life evolved into a routine that included training, a job, school, and the connections that I had developed over the years. Not only did I become stronger physically, but I also became stronger mentally, and it was all because of the man who had taken me under his wing and provided me with a sense of purpose.

The friendship that I shared with Mike and Winston became stronger over those five years. It wasn't simply that we went to the gym together or worked out together; we were a team, and we were each encouraging the other to improve. Regardless of the achievements he had achieved in the past, Winston never failed to amaze me with his admirable humility. In spite of the fact that he was associated with legendary figures, he never boasted or took himself too seriously. From his perspective, every one of us was only a person with our paths and struggles to overcome.

It was because of him that I became a better person. Winston had saved my life in ways that he would never completely comprehend, and I knew that I would always remember the lessons that he had taught me.

# Chapter – 7
# Pivotal Time

My father was unhappy with the direction of my life. He didn't want me to go to the gym, practice martial arts, or clean the dishes. According to him, these mediocre sports and an odd job were bringing shame to him and his family. However, he always wanted me to follow in his footsteps, which he meant to work a job that has job security and is not seasonal.

He hadn't liked me since my birth. He was always against my desires and will. According to him, I was a mistake and a bad soul. He never tried to help me out, but he considered it his right to retaliate for everything I did. Once in life, he did a favor for me, or it was my luck. I'm still not sure.

My father used to work in Nortel as a supervisor. Many of his friends who used to work there used to know me well, probably in good words.

I was following my passion, but I was well aware that training and cleaning dishes were not permanent and didn't pay well.

One bright evening in 1988, I received a call from the union department of Nortel. There was a job opening related to communication tech. Without any second thought, I accepted that offer just to make my father proud, as they were giving me better money than my odd jobs.

Prior to my joining Nortel, when my family learned about the job offer I accepted, my father said to me, "I worked hard to make a name for myself; don't use my name to advance."

His harsh comments devested me, but the hope in my mother's eyes for me was entirely different, and a spark motivated me to work.

On the first day on the job, I was a bit hesitant, with mixed reactions about what to do and what not to do. I aligned myself with my father's friend, who showed me how to do everything to survive in the communication world. He was the one who supported me there in the competitive company.

Actually, Nortel was a telecommunication company with around 50,000 employees available worldwide.

On the other hand, I didn't regret switching my job while being away from my passion for gym and martial arts, as I was about to expand my horizons. This was the best motivation in my life.

I took all my prior experiences from martial arts and everything Winston taught me. Everything I learned within years was transferable to my new working environment, and I had mechanical aptitude.

Back in memory lane, when I was in high school, I was always taking shop classes and working on my motorcycle and fixing motors. I was set to make my name with the company as a communication technician. I have been a technical person since childhood.

I worked hard with full dedication and made all ends meet. For the next few years, I traveled the world installing equipment for Nortel. I traveled to Canada, the US, Europe, Brazil, and the Caribbean. The Caribbean was the best place, a place where I enjoyed working with massive experience.

Because of my hectic schedule with Nortel, I was totally immersed in my job; I had no time for the gym. I used to miss my obsession, but working and earning a great deal of wages was also necessary.

I was entirely occupied with my new life. From time to time, Winston used to call me just to talk and check if I was fine. He was always there to help and always used to ask on calls whether I needed help or not; he used to mention, "Son, remember you have my back; I am always there for you." Actually, he was genuinely concerned about me; if he called me son he considered me as one.

It was my second year when I was away from gym. I was back into drug consumption. One night, my friends from work and I were walking past this club with a huge line, and I heard, "Randy!"

When I turned around, it was Mike from the gym. I was super excited. So I went to see him, and he asked me why he hadn't seen me at the gym. I told him it was because of work. We talked for a couple of minutes, which seemed to be an hour, cherishing old times. He thanked me for everything that I did for him and all the encouragement that I gave him. I told him, "That's what brothers do for each other."

Mike told me that he had enrolled in culinary school. I was so happy to listen as he pursued his passion; at least he got the change he wanted to make.

After a meaningful conversation, as I was about to depart, he gave me a VIP entry into the club. My friends were shocked at our treatment; I jokingly said, "That's my brother."

On the alternate day, our friends went to the club with the VIP entry given by Mike as he was still working as a security guard. The same night, after a couple of hours, a former gang member walked into the club. Times when I was into drugs. It's been 5 years since we talked, and we resumed back up right where we left off. Letting go of all the bad things and becoming friends all over again.

One night, a year later, my friend told me that he was fed up with shaking down people and doing drugs.

With his confession, I realized that I had relapsed back into the old lifestyle through association and told him, "That's it, we are walking away from this, and I am going to take you along with me."

My friend didn't respond. At the same when this man entered the bar, we both knew him from the past. Without wasting any time, he drew a gun and shot my friend in the head. I was in shock at what just happened in front of me within the blink of an eye. I was trying to figure out why the gunman said in a hateful voice, "You're next," and left.

Police questioned me, and I told them that the gunman was a random person and I hadn't seen him before. To avoid legal procedure and ending up in prison, I didn't tell what the gunman told me.

After seeing my friend being shot, I went into a depression for a while, questioning why not me? Why was he shot? Even I can also be at his place. That was the moment that shocked me to the core and provoked me to quit the intake of drugs.

I confined myself to the family priest, Father Victor, and told him that I knew the person who shorted my friend as he was in the revival gang during our teenage days.

Father Victor told me that I was sparred because God had bigger plans for me and that I should use my platform to help others.

The next day, after the family priest reflected on the situation, a song came on the radio from Michael Jackson's "Man in the Mirror." One verse that resonated with me,

"I'm starting with the man in the mirror.

I'm asking him to change his ways.

And no message could've been any clearer.

If they wanna make the world a better place

Take a look at yourself and then make a change."

The gang wanted to retaliate against the man and sought to kill him; I thought about the crossroads. Do I want to avenge a person's death by taking another, or do I walk away and be that man? I always envisioned myself being, so I walked away for good; if I got killed, so be it; I didn't care.

I was struggling with the death of my friend and job, but I wanted a person who knew me well. After 4 to 5 years, I went back to Winston's Gym but found an empty office building, as he had moved. I had not been in contact with him for so long.

So, I had to join another gym, remembering all he had taught me, and resumed training while working at Nortel. I built a huge wall to protect myself. I had to make some serious changes and figure them out on my own.

I was transferred to the plant with Nortel, and I tried to find Winston. I found out there was a managerial position coming up soon, so I attended a night school in Management course at Concordia. I excelled in accounting as my mother was a bookkeeper, so balance sheets came easy for me; I was around it all my life, helping her at her office. She gave up her career in the early 90s for my father's care as he was negotiating his health; he was unable to travel for long as he was suffering from cancer. For two years, I was a manager. On the other hand, she was running her own business, but she sold it without a second thought to be with my father. For my father, Nortel was his life, whereas hockey and drink were the second priority, and family was the least.

As I moved up the chain of command with Nortel, my father commented to me, "You'll never be me." He could have said, "I am proud of you and all your accomplishments."

"I never wanted you to be my father," I told him, "I don't want to be you; I want to blaze my own path in life and make a difference."

One day, when I was visiting the hospital to see my dying father, I stopped in this bakery a block away to get a muffin. As I entered, I saw Mike behind the counter, I was happy to see him; he confessed to me that he had pursued his dream and opened up his own business and thanked me for all the inspiration that I gave him years ago. My heart was filled with happiness; this gave me a sense of joy. My mother told me he wants you to apologize to him.

The most confusing part of life was when my father was on his deathbed; he wanted me to apologize to him for all the bad behaviors that I've done in the past. My father never reciprocated his behavior by hitting my mother.

My father died in September 1998, and he was retired from Nortel six months prior to his death.

However, I was moving ahead in life, and Nortel offered me a position at a different plant that I accepted in 1998. After a few months at the new plant, I was promoted to final inspection with Doris. Doris and I were a team; she was my right hand, and I was her left.

After being introduced to everyone, I met Lin and tried to talk to her, but she didn't want to, as she had nothing to do with me. Somebody instructed me to stay away from her, as she was off limits and going through a bad breakup.

Time changed, and a few months later, we started talking about our interests. We were both having a good time together, and a comfort zone was developed between us.

A week later, she approached me during work and said, "A guy is staring with piercing eyes at me and making me feel uncomfortable."

So I approached him and said, "Why are you staring at my girlfriend?" At that time, we were not in a relationship but I portrayed in front of the man that we are. I further added, "Stop doing this, or I will take you out back and beat you up."

The piercing-eyed guy went over to Lin and apologized to her; she was confused as to why he did so.

A few minutes later, I passed by and said, "You owe me a beer."

Later on, after work, we were at the bar; Lin approached the table with beer and said, "I promised you a beer here."

I was amazed that she did as she sat next to me. She inquired about what I said to that person. I told her that man would never bug you again. She was amazed at how calm, cool, and collected I was. She thought it was an act, and I told her, "I went through my metamorphosis years ago; what you see is what you get."

As time went on, I let her into my heart, I let my guard down, and I fell in love with her. I knew that she was the best thing that ever happened to me. Two years later, we flew to Las Vegas and got married in a Chapel in 2000 and have been married since.

In early 2003, my employment at Nortel was terminated due to a restructuring process, and I eventually declared Chapter 11 in 2009.

During my 15 years working in the telecommunications industry, I honed a variety of skills that shaped me into an effective manager. Among the most valuable was communication—the ability to clearly articulate needs and expectations, which is essential for success in any role. I learned the importance of teamwork, recognizing that collective effort, with each member contributing meaningfully, drives the efficiency of the whole.

I mastered the art of engagement, understanding that meaningful conversations are as much about attentive listening as they are about speaking. By echoing and building on others' thoughts, I ensured that my colleagues felt heard and valued. Training became a significant part of my role as I guided and educated others, effectively transferring knowledge and fostering a positive learning environment. This naturally extended to teaching, where I utilized techniques that helped individuals achieve their desired outcomes.

Encouragement was at the heart of my leadership style—I always made it a point to recognize and credit the great work of my team. Additionally, coaching and mentoring played a pivotal role in my approach. I encouraged individuals to take ownership of their responsibilities, helping them grow and reach their full potential, both professionally and personally. These skills not only defined my career but also profoundly shaped my philosophy as a leader.

The year 2003 was heavy as I had the responsibility of my mother and Lin. Sometimes, we are just helpless.

Later, in 2004, Lin was also terminated from Nortel. The main reason many employees were terminated was that they were downsizing. As they were not evaluating with time, they were not cutting rates, whereas many companies in competition were opened with minimal rates.

# Chapter – 8
# Taking Care of Mom

After Nortel terminated my employment in 2003, I spent two years doing odd jobs to support Lin and myself. It wasn't easy, but I believed in pushing through life's challenges. Eventually, in late 2005, I secured a position in the shipping and receiving department at the Post Office. It wasn't glamorous, but it was stable, and stability was exactly what we needed at the time.

Since my father's passing, my mother has leaned on Lin and me for emotional support. While she managed her own finances, her frequent tears and conversations about how much she missed my father puzzled me. Why would she miss a man who was hardly present and, when he was, often hurtful? Yet, I didn't voice these thoughts. I simply listened, offering her the understanding she needed.

One evening, as we sat in her cozy living room, my mother began reminiscing about Puerto Rico. "Your father worked there for ten years with Nortel," she said softly, her voice tinged with nostalgia. "I gave up my business to join him. We lived in a condo by the beach. Those were... interesting times."

"You gave up so much for him," I said, a hint of frustration in my tone.

She shrugged. "That's what marriage is, Randy. Compromise."

I didn't fully agree, but I didn't push back. Instead, we talked about Puerto Rico—the memories, the places, and the people. Tony, the owner of Alambique, a vibrant outdoor bar by the beach, came up often in our conversations. Tony had been like family to me during my visits, always greeting me with warmth and solidarity.

Lin, who had been quietly listening to us chat, suddenly said, "Where is Puerto Rico, exactly? I want to see it!"

Her enthusiasm caught me off guard but delighted me. "You really want to go?" I asked, my face lighting up.

"Of course! Let's visit all these places you and your mom keep talking about," she replied, smiling.

A few months later, as our eighth wedding anniversary approached, I surprised Lin with tickets to San Juan. I couldn't wait to revisit the island and share my cherished memories with her.

The moment we landed in Puerto Rico, I felt a wave of nostalgia wash over me. The warm breeze carried the scent of the ocean, and the vibrant colors of the buildings felt like a welcome embrace. Within an hour of checking into our hotel, we made our way to Alambique.

As we entered, Tony was behind the bar. The moment he saw me, his face lit up. He rushed around the bar, and we embraced like long-lost brothers.

"Long time no see, Brother!" Tony exclaimed, his booming voice filled with joy.

"It's been too long, Tony," I replied, grinning ear to ear.

Lin watched our reunion in awe. "It's like no time has passed," she remarked.

I introduced her to Tony, who shook her hand warmly. "Welcome to the family," he said.

I explained to Lin, "In Puerto Rico, a handshake like that means you're family. If arms are crossed, well... get ready for a fight."

She laughed, clearly amused but also fascinated by the culture.

A few days later, while we were enjoying the historic beauty of Old San Juan, we decided to stop by Alambique again. As we settled in, a man entered the bar, and Tony's demeanor immediately changed. His arms crossed, his face hardened.

Lin nudged me. "Look at Tony. What's going on?"

I glanced over and saw the tension. "That guy must have caused trouble before," I said.

Approaching Tony, I asked, "What's the story?"

Tony sighed. "Last night, this guy started a fight outside. He's not welcome here."

"Want me to handle it?" I offered.

Tony nodded, so I walked up to the man. "Your presence isn't welcome here," I said firmly.

"All I want is one beer," he replied, clearly trying to defuse the situation.

Tony signaled to the bartender, granting him one drink. The man quietly finished his beer and left, muttering under his breath. As soon as he was gone, the bar erupted in cheers.

Tony handed me a beer and said, "Thanks, Brother. You're family, always."

"That's what family is for," I replied, smiling.

When we returned home, we couldn't stop talking about the trip. Lin and I shared our adventures with my mother, who listened with a mix of pride and nostalgia.

"Did you explore the whole island?" she asked.

"Not yet," I admitted. "But we'll go back."

The following year, we decided to take my mother with us to Puerto Rico. It was my way of thanking her for her unwavering support and being the guiding light in my life. We booked her a flight and arranged for her to stay in a room next to ours.

Seeing my mother in Puerto Rico was magical. She became our personal tour guide, sharing stories and memories at every turn. One day, we rented a Jeep and drove to Rincon, a small town on the western tip of the island, to watch the sunset. The view was breathtaking, and the joy on my mother's face made the trip worthwhile.

The next day, she took us on a tour of the Bacardi distillery. As we drove back to the hotel, we passed a bar she recognized. "That used to be Duffy's," she said, her voice tinged with reminiscence. "Your father and I used to come here sometimes."

We decided to stop for a drink. While we were there, a man approached our table and greeted my mother warmly. It was Steve, an old friend of my father's. They spent the next hour reminiscing, their laughter filling the bar.

Afterward, my mother admitted, "I was hesitant about coming back here, but I needed this. I needed closure."

Her words stayed with me. It reminded me that even the most painful memories could lead to healing if faced with courage and love.

As the years passed, my mother became increasingly dependent on Lin and me. She was aging, and though she was fiercely independent, I could see her leaning on us more and more.

One evening, as I was helping her organize some paperwork, she said, "You know, Randy, I'm proud of you. You've come so far."

Those words did catch me off guard, but my mother was always my rock, encouraging me to excel. My father never gave me the same accolades or spoke highly of me as he did with other people. I always knew how she felt, but it was nice to hear. "Thanks, Mom," I said, my voice thick with emotion. "I wouldn't be here without you."

She smiled. "You've always had a good heart. Even when you stumbled, you found your way back."

Caring for my mother wasn't always easy, but it was a responsibility I embraced wholeheartedly. She had sacrificed so much for our family, and it was my turn to give back. Lin was my rock through it all, offering support and compassion every step of the way.

Looking back, those years were some of the most challenging and rewarding of my life. They taught me the true meaning of family—the bonds we build, the sacrifices we make, and the love that carries us through the hardest times.

Even now, as I write these words, I can still hear my mother's voice, filled with wisdom and love, reminding me to always keep moving forward. And for her, I always will.

# Chapter – 9
# Competition Days

When passion becomes an obsession, no one can stop you. I had to learn that truth the hard way, through years of stumbling and getting back up again. Gym and martial arts had always been my anchor, my sanctuary, my way of making sense of the world. But there were times when I drifted away from them, times when drugs replaced discipline, and the darkness clouded my vision.

The death of my closest friend in front of my eyes shook me awake. It wasn't just a wake-up call—it was a shock that flipped my world upside down. I quit drugs. It wasn't easy, but I had made my choice. I embraced the gym again, as well as martial arts, and set my sights on creating a healthy, purposeful life.

During those early days of reclaiming my identity, I worked odd jobs to support my family while simultaneously training at the gym. To make a little extra cash, I started teaching martial arts to individuals who were eager to learn. Training others reignited something in me, a spark of my old self, the one who had once dreamed big.

One day at the gym, I overheard a group of guys talking about various organizations and competitions they aspired to join. Their excitement was contagious. It reminded me of my old dreams—dreams I had almost buried under years of bad choices. That's when I realized that dreams have no expiration date. Even Mike inspired me to pursue my dreams.

I remembered my old friend Paul from Winston's gym, who had made it big in the bodybuilding world. For years, I had seen his name in magazines, and every time, I'd tell people, "I knew that guy!" Of course, most of them laughed it off as if I was making it up. Their skepticism stung, but it pushed me to dig deeper. I did my research, and sure enough, it was the same Paul.

By 2007, Paul had founded the WBFF (World Beauty Fitness & Fashion), an organization that was making waves in the fitness world.

He had created a division specifically for male fitness models, recognizing that not everyone could—or wanted to—be a massive bodybuilder.

In 2009, I took a leap of faith and registered as a fitness model for an event in the WBFF. I didn't know where this would lead, but I was ready to find out. While standing in line during registration, I caught a familiar face out of the corner of my eye. It was Paul.

I hesitated for a moment, wondering if he would even remember me. Summoning my courage, I called out, "Hey, Paul, long time no see! It's Randy—remember Winston's gym?"

His reaction was immediate—a wide smile followed by a hearty hug. "Randy! Of course, I remember you!" he exclaimed, introducing me to everyone around him, including his wife. "This guy knows Winston!" he said proudly.

We spent the next hour catching up. Seeing Paul reminded me of the first time he walked into Winston's gym—a shy, skinny kid 6"1" and 175 pounds with big dreams. In a year, he had transformed into a confident, muscular powerhouse, weighing an impressive 250 pounds. I had been envious of the attention Winston gave him back then, but I understood why. Paul was destined for greatness, and Winston was simply nurturing his potential.

Inspired by Paul's vision, I decided to compete. My first competition was a whirlwind of emotions—nervousness, excitement, and sheer determination. When a local newspaper wrote a small piece about me, I was on cloud nine. It felt like validation like I was finally on the right path.

One evening, as I was leaving the gym, a police car pulled up. My stomach sank. "Not again," I muttered to myself, half-expecting trouble. But when the officer stepped out, I recognized him immediately—it was the same cop who had helped me out as a troubled youth.

"Randy!" he called out, his voice filled with pride. "I've been following your journey. You've turned your life around, and I couldn't be prouder."

His words hit me hard. He went on to tell me how his son, whom I had trained in martial arts years ago, was now a firefighter. "Your encouragement made all the difference," he said. "You've shown people what it means to lift others up."

Those words stayed with me. They reaffirmed my belief that we all have the power to make a difference.

In 2009, Father Victor from my church approached me with an idea. "Randy," he said, "would you consider speaking to some of our troubled youth? Share your story with them. It might help."

I hesitated at first. What did I have to offer these kids? But I agreed, knowing how much the encouragement of others had shaped my own life.

The first few sessions were tough. Many of the kids were distant, lost in their worlds. But then I met Josh, an 11-year-old boy battling leukemia. Despite his illness, he had a spark—a belief that anything was possible.

I opened up to Josh about my struggles, telling him that with a little encouragement, he could achieve anything. I invited him to one of my competitions, and he came, beaming with excitement. Backstage, he watched in awe as I prepared for the stage. "You're like a superhero," he said, dubbing me "Randyman."

Six months later, Josh passed away. His parents thanked me for being a source of inspiration during his final days. Their gratitude was bittersweet, a reminder of the impact we can have on others, even in the smallest ways.

In 2010, I set my sights on competing at the WBFF Worlds. Training at Gold's Gym, I met Hector, an MMA instructor who reignited my interest in martial arts. Though I had to focus on the competition first, I knew martial arts would always be part of my life.

The next two years were a blur of intense training, competitions, and personal growth. Paul and his wife were incredibly supportive, often going out of their way to help me. Through the WBFF, I met amazing competitors, many of whom became lifelong friends.

Throughout this journey, I often thought of Winston, the man who had set me on this path. I heard he was facing health challenges and wished I could thank him personally for everything he had done for me.

"Next time you talk to Winston, say hi for me," I told Paul.

"I will," he promised. And I believed him.

Looking back, the years of competing were about more than just trophies or recognition. They were about proving to myself—and to the world—that change is possible. That no matter how far you've fallen, you can rise again.

The gym and martial arts weren't just hobbies; they were lifelines. They gave me discipline, purpose, and a platform to inspire others. Whether it was mentoring a young boy like Josh, reconnecting with old friends like Paul, or simply being present for my family, every step of this journey was a reminder of what truly matters.

Competition days taught me that passion can transform lives—not just my own but everyone I touched along the way. And for that, I will always be grateful.

# Chapter – 10
# Full Circle

In early 2015, I was transferred to a new location at the post office called Gateway Processing Plant. It was a decent place, and the people there were welcoming. One day, during my break, I noticed a familiar face across the room; I am good at remembering the faces of the people who even once had crossed my way. I couldn't immediately place her, but something about her struck a chord. Without much thought, I approached her.

"Hi, I'm Randy," I said warmly.

She looked up, slightly puzzled but polite, and introduced herself. "I'm Catherine, but everyone calls me Cat."

As we exchanged pleasantries, something clicked. "Wait," I said, my mind connecting the dots. "You're Hector's wife, aren't you? From Gold's Gym?"

"Yes, you are right, Randy."

"It's been five years; Hector offered me training in the MMA."

She smiled, and we both started a deep conversation. During our conversation, I jokingly said, "Maybe four of us should go out for dinner."

Her expression changed instantly. A faint smile lingered, but then her face clouded over. Tears welled up in her eyes, and she quickly looked away. I felt an uncomfortable knot form in my stomach.

"I'm sorry," she said, her voice breaking. "I had to take time off to care for Hector before he passed away from ALS."

The words hit me like a freight train. "Oh my God, Cat, I'm so sorry. I had no idea. He was such a great guy. If there's anything I can do—anything at all—please don't hesitate to ask."

Cat nodded, still visibly emotional. "Thank you. It's been a tough few years, but I'm trying to move forward."

Actually, ALS: Amyotrophic Lateral Sclerosis is a disease that progressively paralyzes people because the brain is no longer able to communicate with the muscles of the body that we are typically able to move at will. Over time, as the muscles of the body break down, someone living with ALS will lose the ability to walk, talk, eat, swallow, and eventually breathe. I could sympathize with Cat as my sister-in-law's husband had the same disease.

Over the weeks that followed, we began talking more. The Cat would often open up about Hector's battle with ALS, a cruel disease that takes everything from a person piece by piece. I truly listened because I knew that's what she needed most.

"You know, Randy," she said one day, "you're easy to talk to. You never interrupt or try to fix things. You… listen."

I smiled and shrugged. "Sometimes that's all anyone needs."

Through our conversations, I learned how deeply Cat had sacrificed for Hector. She gave up a promising singing career in Europe to help him run his MMA school.

"I've never regretted it," she said. "Hector was my everything. If he were still alive, you two would have been best friends. You're so alike—same energy, same passion."

Her words stayed with me. One evening, I invited Cat to a coffee shop to meet my wife, Lin. The two hit it off immediately, and Cat became a close family friend from that day forward.

About six months later, while scrolling through Facebook, I saw a post that stopped me. My old mentor Winston was hosting an event in Cobourg on October 10. My heart raced as memories flooded back. Without hesitation, I reserved a ticket, determined to surprise him.

The event day arrived, and as I stepped into the venue, my eyes scanned the room. And then I saw him. Winston. He stood about twenty feet away, chatting with someone, looking just as I remembered but a little older. Our eyes met, and it felt like time had rewound at that moment.

I walked over, my heart pounding. "You might not remember me, but…"

Before I could finish, Winston's face lit up. "Randy," he said, his voice full of warmth. "Welcome home, son."

We both hugged for a long time. I was overjoyed that Winston recognized me instantly, even after 20 years.

His words hit me like a wave of emotion. "You remembered," I said, my voice barely above a whisper. We embraced, and for a moment, nothing else mattered.

"I've always wondered what happened to my star protégé," Winston said. "I'm so glad to see you again."

We spent hours catching up after the competition. I told him everything—the highs, the lows, the lessons I'd learned along the way.

"You saved my life, Winston," I said, my voice cracking. "What you did for me all those years ago… I wouldn't be here without you."

He nodded, visibly moved. "You've come a long way, Randy. I'm proud of you."

Before we parted that night, Winston said, "This was the best birthday gift I've had in years." His birthday had been just five days earlier, on October 5. It felt like fate.

During my conversations with Winston, I inquired, "Did Paul ever say hi to you?"

Winston replied, "No, I have no idea what you are talking about. Yes, he did call him up, but he never said anything about you; everything was about Paul."

I was so disappointed in Paul. Winston told me if he had known that I was competing in Paul's organization, maybe he'd be in the audience or backstage to cheer me on.

In April 2016, I competed in Winston's next competition. The moment I stepped on stage, I spotted him in the crowd. He stood behind me, clapping and smiling as I completed my posing routine. When I stepped off stage, I couldn't hold back my tears.

A host approached me with a microphone. "Randy, who would you say has been your biggest mentor?"

Without hesitation, I pointed to Winston. "This man believed in me when I didn't believe in myself. Whatever I am today is because of him."

I saw the pride in Winston's eyes as he came to find me backstage. "You did it, Randy," he said, his voice filled with emotion. "You've reached your potential, and I couldn't be prouder."

That moment meant everything to me. To receive Winston's approval felt like getting the blessing of a father—something I'd never had. It was as if my journey had come full circle.

Over the next few years, I attended many events with Winston and his incredible crew. Each competition felt like a reunion, celebrating how far we'd all come. I forged lifelong friendships with people like Michael, John, Barrymore, Wesley, Greg, Terry, and Alvin.

But it was Winston who remained at the heart of it all. He'd judged legends like Arnold Schwarzenegger and Frank Zane, yet he always made time for me. His belief in me was a gift I'd treasure forever.

To this day, I still get a tear in my eye when I think about Winston's unwavering support. It wasn't just about bodybuilding; it was about life. Winston taught me that the people who cross our paths do so for a reason. They shape, guide, and help us become who we're meant to be.

In the end, it wasn't about the trophies or the accolades. It was about the connections, the lessons, and the journey. And for that, I'll always be grateful.

WINSTON ROBERTS
ton Roberts
oberts.com
69
MAX
SUPPLEMENTS
GNC
LIVE WELL

WINSTON ROBERTS
WINSTON ROBERTS
GNC
LIVE WELL
ALLMAX

# Chapter – 11
# Passing the Torch

On August 26,2017, Winston scheduled a competition under his name, "Winston Roberts Open," which was his last competition. That day was my birthday, but I didn't tell him. I was so proud and excited to spend time on my special day with him, as I've always thought of him as my father figure.

After the competition, when we were about to meet again, I saw Winston coming, I was happy, but with his expression, I could recognize that something was bothering him.

"Hey, Winston!"

Instead of replying to my greetings, he said firmly. "I am mad at you."

I frowned and started thinking about what I had done that made him mad.

I asked him, "Why?"

"You didn't tell me it is your birthday."

As I was about to say a word, Winston continued, "Luckily, I came to know about your birthday through the wishes you received on your Facebook when I was scrolling."

I breathed relief, grinned, and said, "There's no other place that I'd rather be than right next to you on my birthday."

He was so overwhelmed with my words that he hugged me. Winston made a special statement that it was my birthday and how happy he was to spend it with me. Everyone around us wished me, and I was on the seventh sky, as it was the best birthday and probably the last too.

One thing I learned from Winston during his speech to the athletes was that were competing; he always made it a fact to acknowledge the backstage staff as he always does. For him, success was not a one-man show; it was a team effort.

On 3rd December of 2017, two weeks prior to Winston's passing, I texted him, "Hi Winston, hope all is well with you? It's been a while since we've talked, just touching base with you to let you know you always have a special place in my heart."

He texted back, "Thanks, Randy. The same is true here. I think of you all the time. Thanks for being you. Cheers!"

His words touched me deeply, and I called him right away. He said, "I am really proud of the man you are and the man you became!" Winston continued on by saying, "The reason that I took an interest in you at my gym years ago was that you remind me of me; we both wear our hearts on sleeves, interacting with others and how you could break down, describe exercises, or find an alternative just like me which makes you a very special trainer!"

I happily responded to him, "You've made a huge impact on my life; what can I do for you?"

He told me, "I 've empowered you with a wealth of information in bodybuilding along with your extensive knowledge of martial arts; now it's your time to impact others and mentor and coach them to be the best person they can be!"

A meaningful and confessing conversation between us still motivated me whenever I was down. I am glad I had the courage to speak my heart out, and he did the same.

Two weeks later, on December 22, 2017, Winston passed away, I was devastated. I was unable to figure out what had happened to me, as I denied the reality; after around two decades, we met, and now he is no more with me; I have left again without a father.

A few days later, I gathered courage and posted farewell words. It stated, "It was a very somber day as we said goodbye to a great man, legend, mentor, and a very special friend Winston  Roberts.

Oh my drive home, I was reminded of a story when I was in Winston's gym in Montreal many years ago. I was in Winston's office and in walk in Joe and Ben Weider (I was in disbelief Ben and Joe are sitting next to a 16 year old kid) and sat next to me and started talking about bringing Lee Haney to the gym I was thinking yeah right

Mr. Olympia is coming out Winston's gym. Sure, enough the next week in walks Lee, larger than life to talk to us about training, life and his experiences.

I stood in the back looking at the love and respect that Lee showed Winston, it was a truly humble experience.

A week later, I brought my two cousins into Winston's, Bernie Tapp and Patrick Rehel, to work out; Winston passed by me and told my two cousins they were going to be put through their paces and told me to take it easy on them, next day they couldn't move!

Thank you for the great memories! Miss you and Love you!!"

I received condolences from past superstars of the IFBB like Lee Haney, Vince Taylor, Shawn Ray etc.

Winston was suffering from cancer, but he didn't let me know what he was going through.

During the next 8 months after Winston passed away, my mother was in and out of the hospital as she was diagnosed with cancer a year prior, but she was getting worse from different chemo treatments that she received.

During the time of my travels to see my mother in the hospital, Cat was concerned about me, and she texted me every day to make sure that I was okay emotionally and physically. In the last three weeks, while in the hospital, my mother requested that one of her best friends and sister-in-law, Aunt Estelle, be by her side while she battled cancer and be a source of comfort to myself and my sister.

On July 18, 2018, my mother passed away; I cried because my mother and Winston had a huge impact on my life. Now, both are gone physically, but their spirit still lives on. With my mother's demise, I was shattered and completely lost in my world. With Lin by my side and good friends like Cat and others who have really helped me during the worst phase of my life. It took me around a year to be normal, but still, my life is incomplete without Winston and my mother.

# Chapter – 12
# Full Circle: A Life Reclaimed

Life has a way of moving forward, whether we're ready or not. Time doesn't wait for anyone. People come and go, and circumstances change, but the experiences that shape us and the lessons we carry remain. As I stand where I am today, I know that no one can ever replace the people who meant the most to me—my mentor, Winston, my mother, and those who guided me through my darkest moments. Their presence in my life was a gift, and their absence reminds me that nothing lasts forever.

One day, I found myself walking through a mall, aimlessly window shopping, when I heard a voice call out, "Randy, how are you?"

I turned to see a man with a familiar face, but I couldn't immediately place him. He recognized the confusion on my face and chuckled. After a few hints and references, I finally realized who he was—a former gang member and an old friend from my past. We had started using drugs together in our younger years, but while I had managed to escape that life, it seemed he was still caught in its grip.

We spoke briefly, recalling about old times, though our paths had taken drastically different turns. As we talked, he repeatedly insisted that we grab a drink together. Then, almost as if he had been waiting for the right moment, he revealed that he only had $20 to his name— not enough to buy the drink he wanted.

Without hesitation, he asked, "Randy, could you lend me some money? Just a little. I'll pay you back in a few days."

He was an old friend I had once trusted, so I gave him the money. But those "few days" never came, and I never saw that money again. It wasn't about the money, though—it was about the realization that some people never change. He had become dependent on others to survive, refusing to take control of his own life. I had walked away from that world, but he was still trapped.

Sometimes, I drive by the old neighborhoods I once thought I ruled. The faces have changed, but the stories remain the same. The people I used to admire, those I once wanted to be like, are either on welfare, still doing drugs, or hustling to survive. Some are in jail. Others are dead. And every time I pass by, I think, "That could have been me."

My journey has been full of ups and downs, but through small, determined steps, I climbed my way out. When I stood at the crossroads, I listened. I followed the guidance of those who believed in me, who saw potential in me when I couldn't see it in myself. Without them, I don't know where I would be today.

I've learned over the years that everyone needs someone to believe in them. It could be a parent, a sibling, a mentor, or even a stranger. My grandmother, whom I called Nana, was one of those people for me. So was Winston. Someone who listens, supports, and pushes you forward can make all the difference between failure and success.

My Life's Formulas for Success:

Stop regretting the past: You can't change what has happened, but you can learn from it and use those lessons to move forward.

Take responsibility for your actions: Life will throw obstacles your way, but how you respond to them defines you.

Find happiness within yourself: True happiness isn't found in external validation or material success—it comes from within. Once you understand that, everything else falls into place.

Believe in your inner strength: You are stronger than you think. Trust your abilities, embrace your resilience, and understand that every setback is an opportunity to learn and grow.

Stop worrying about the unknown: Fear of the future only holds you back. Trust in yourself and your ability to handle whatever comes your way.

Today, I stand proud of what I have achieved. There is still so much more to do, but I have no regrets about how my life has turned out. I've met incredible individuals who have helped shape me into the man I am today. I am happily married, surrounded by positive people, and dedicated to giving back.

Through my business, I actively engage with people who seek to improve themselves. My website, Randy-Fitness.com, is a platform where I offer guidance, support, and training, helping others unlock their potential.

I have turned my lifelong passion into something tangible—a small business, Private Dojo, and Studio Gym. As a certified Kickboxing Instructor and Personal Trainer, I now help others find their strength, just as I once found mine.

This journey has come full circle from a lost boy caught in addiction and self-destruction to a man who stands strong, confident, and driven. The road wasn't easy, but it was worth every struggle every lesson, and every moment of growth.

If there is one thing I want people to take from my story, it is this: no matter where you come from or how lost you feel, you always have the power to turn your life around. All you need is the courage to take that first step.

And for that, I am forever grateful.